CONTENTS

INTRODUCTION

Brief Overview of WIX

WIX is a leading cloud-based development platform that allows users to create and manage their websites effortlessly. Launched in 2006, WIX has gained immense popularity for its user-friendly interface, enabling both beginners and professionals to design stunning websites without the need for extensive coding knowledge. The platform offers a range of customizable templates, ensuring that users can tailor their websites to suit their unique needs. WIX also provides a drag-and-drop editor, making the process of building and updating websites intuitive and accessible. With features like WIX ADI (Artificial Design Intelligence), users can even have the platform generate a personalized website based on their preferences.

One of the key advantages of WIX is its versatility. Whether you are a small business owner, a creative professional, or someone looking to establish an online presence, WIX provides the tools and resources to make it happen. The platform supports various industries, allowing users to create websites for e-commerce, portfolios, blogs, and more. Additionally, WIX offers a range of add-ons and apps that enhance the functionality of websites, such as e-commerce capabilities, social media integrations, and marketing tools.

Key Features of WIX:

1. **User-Friendly Interface:** WIX's intuitive drag-and-drop editor makes website creation accessible to users with little to no coding experience.

2. **Customizable Templates:** A wide array of templates catering to different industries ensures that users can find a design that aligns with their vision.

3. **WIX ADI:** The platform's Artificial Design Intelligence can generate a personalized website by asking users a series of questions about their preferences and needs.

4. **Versatility:** WIX caters to various industries, allowing users to create websites for different purposes, including business, portfolio, and personal blogs.

5. **Add-Ons and Apps:** WIX's App Market offers a range of add-ons and apps that enhance website functionality, such as e-commerce features and marketing tools.

In summary, WIX has become a go-to platform for individuals and businesses looking to establish a compelling online presence. Its user-friendly interface, customizable templates, and versatile features make it a valuable tool for web development.

Importance of Creating a Website for Beginners

In the digital age, having an online presence is crucial for individuals and businesses alike. For beginners, the process of creating a website may seem daunting, but the benefits far outweigh the initial challenges. Here's a comprehensive look at why creating a website is essential for beginners entering the online space.

1. Personal Branding:

In today's competitive world, personal branding is key to standing out. A website serves as your digital identity, allowing you to showcase your skills, achievements, and personality. It's a platform where you can control the narrative and present yourself in the best light.

2. Professional Credibility:

Whether you're an individual freelancer or a small business owner, having a professional-looking website adds credibility. Clients and customers often use the internet to research and validate businesses or individuals before making decisions. A well-designed website signals professionalism and competence.

3. Networking Opportunities:

A website provides a centralized hub for your online presence. It becomes a powerful tool for networking, connecting with peers, potential clients, or collaborators. It also opens doors to opportunities you might not have encountered otherwise.

4. Showcasing Portfolio and Work:

For artists, photographers, writers, and other creatives, a website acts as a virtual portfolio. It allows you to showcase your work to a global audience, attracting potential clients or employers who can easily explore your talent and skills.

5. Learning and Growth:

The process of creating a website itself is a valuable learning experience. Beginners can acquire new skills, from basic web design to content creation and digital marketing. This continuous learning process contributes to personal and professional growth.

6. Global Reach:

Unlike traditional methods of advertising or self-promotion, a website provides a global reach. Your audience is not limited by geographical boundaries, allowing you to connect with people from different parts of the world who share similar interests or professional goals.

7. Cost-Effective Marketing:

Compared to traditional marketing methods, maintaining a website is cost-effective. It serves as an ever-present marketing tool, accessible to anyone with an internet connection. This is especially advantageous for beginners with limited budgets.

In conclusion, the importance of creating a website for beginners cannot be overstated. It's a transformative step that opens doors to personal and professional opportunities, enhances credibility, and contributes to ongoing learning and growth.

Goals of the Ebook

Creating an ebook is a powerful way to share knowledge, expertise, and insights with a targeted audience. The goals of an ebook can vary based on the author's intentions, but generally, they revolve around providing value, establishing authority, and achieving specific outcomes. Let's delve into the common goals associated with creating an ebook.

1. Providing Value:

The primary goal of any ebook is to provide valuable

content to the readers. Whether it's offering practical tips, in-depth insights, or solutions to common problems, the ebook should leave the audience with a sense of having gained something substantial.

2. Establishing Authority:

An ebook is an excellent tool for establishing the author's authority in a particular niche or industry. By sharing expertise and knowledge, the author positions themselves as a credible source. This can lead to increased trust from the audience and potential opportunities for collaboration or business.

3. Building a Relationship with the Audience:

Ebooks are a means of building a relationship with the audience. Through well-crafted content, the author can connect with readers on a personal level, addressing their needs and concerns. This engagement fosters a sense of community and loyalty.

4. Lead Generation:

Ebooks are often used as a lead generation tool. Authors may offer a free ebook in exchange for the reader's contact information. This not only expands the author's reach but also creates a pool of potential customers or clients for future products or services.

5. Educational Purposes:

Ebooks are an effective medium for educational purposes. Whether it's a how-to guide, a tutorial, or an informative piece, the goal is to educate the audience on a specific topic. This aligns with providing value and building authority.

6. Branding and Visibility:

Publishing an ebook contributes to personal or brand

visibility. It serves as a tangible representation of the author's expertise and can be a powerful tool for brand building. Increased visibility can lead to new opportunities and a broader audience reach.

7. Achieving Specific Outcomes:

Authors often have specific outcomes in mind when creating an ebook. This could include driving traffic to a website, promoting a product or service, or even advocating for a cause. Clearly defining these outcomes helps guide the content and structure of the ebook.

GETTING STARTED WITH WIX

*Signing Up and Creating
an Account*

Creating an account on a platform is the first step towards unlocking a world of possibilities. The process should be seamless, user-friendly, and secure. When it comes to WIX, signing up is a breeze. To begin, visit the WIX website and locate the "Sign Up" or "Get Started" button. Click on it to initiate the account creation process.

Step-by-step guide to account creation

1. **Visit the WIX website**: Open your preferred web browser and navigate to the official WIX website.

2. **Click on "Sign Up" or "Get Started"**: Look for the prominently displayed sign-up button. This is usually located on the homepage.

3. **Provide your email address**: Enter a valid email address that you have access to. This will be your

primary point of contact with WIX.

4. **Create a strong password**: Choose a password that combines letters, numbers, and symbols to enhance security.

5. **Select the type of website you want to create**: WIX offers a variety of templates tailored to different needs, such as business, portfolio, or blog. Choose the one that aligns with your goals.

6. **Answer a few questions**: WIX will ask some basic questions to understand your preferences and requirements better. This helps in recommending suitable templates and features.

7. **Verify your email**: Check your inbox for a verification email from WIX. Click on the verification link to confirm your account.

8. **Complete your profile**: Add essential information to your profile, including your name and any other details relevant to your website.

Congratulations! You've successfully signed up and created your WIX account. Now, let's delve into the next crucial step.

Choosing a suitable plan

WIX offers various plans catering to different user needs. Choosing the right plan is essential for unlocking the platform's full potential. Here are the key options to consider:

1. **Free Plan**: Ideal for beginners or those testing

the waters. It provides basic features and a WIX-branded domain.

2. **Combo Plan**: A great choice for personal use. It removes WIX ads, includes a custom domain, and offers additional storage.

3. **Unlimited Plan**: Suitable for entrepreneurs and freelancers. This plan provides unlimited bandwidth, additional storage, and a Site Booster app.

4. **Pro Plan**: Geared towards small businesses. It includes all the features of the Unlimited Plan plus access to the WIX Logo Maker.

5. **VIP Plan**: The top-tier plan with priority support, VIP access, and a professional site review.

Consider your website's purpose, your budget, and the features required before selecting a plan. Remember, as your needs evolve, you can always upgrade to a more advanced plan.

Navigating the WIX Dashboard

Once your account is set up, you'll find yourself in the WIX dashboard – your command center for website creation and management. Navigating this space efficiently is crucial for a productive experience.

Understanding the interface

WIX's dashboard is designed with user-friendliness in mind. Here's a breakdown of its key components:

1. **Top Bar**: Houses essential shortcuts, including

access to your site's dashboard, Editor, and various settings.

2. **Left-side Menu**: Contains a plethora of options, from managing your site's pages to accessing the WIX App Market.

3. **Site Overview**: Provides an at-a-glance view of your site's performance, visitor statistics, and any notifications.

4. **Editor**: The heart of WIX, where you'll design and customize your website. Accessible from the dashboard.

Key features and tools

WIX offers a robust set of features and tools to empower users in building and maintaining their websites. Here are some standout elements:

1. **WIX ADI (Artificial Design Intelligence)**: Perfect for beginners, it creates a website for you based on your answers to a few questions.

2. **Editor**: A powerful tool allowing full creative control. Drag-and-drop elements, customize layouts, and design every aspect of your site.

3. **WIX App Market**: A treasure trove of apps to enhance your site's functionality. From e-commerce tools to marketing solutions, the App Market has it all.

4. **Blog Manager**: Ideal for those incorporating a blog into their website. Manage posts, categories, and engage with your audience seamlessly.

5. **WIX Ascend**: A suite of marketing tools to boost your online presence. Includes email campaigns,

automations, and social media posting.

Navigating the WIX dashboard becomes an enjoyable experience when you grasp the functionality of these features. Take your time to explore and experiment, and soon you'll be crafting a website that aligns perfectly with your vision.

CHOOSING THE RIGHT TEMPLATE

Exploring WIX Template Options

When it comes to creating a stunning and functional website, WIX stands out as a versatile platform with a plethora of template options. Navigating through the multitude of templates available can be both perplexing and exciting. The first step in this exploration is gaining an overview of the available templates, understanding their features, and then making a well-informed selection based on your specific needs.

Overview of Available Templates

WIX offers a diverse range of templates that cater to various industries and purposes. Whether you're a small business owner, a creative professional, or someone looking to establish an online presence, there's a template for you. The templates are categorized into different themes, such as business, portfolio, e-commerce, and more. Each theme encompasses multiple designs, providing users with ample choices to find the one that resonates with their brand identity.

To add a layer of perplexity, WIX frequently updates its template library, ensuring that users have access to contemporary designs and functionalities. This dynamic nature means that the options are ever-evolving, keeping up with the latest trends in web design. It's not just about choosing a template; it's about selecting one that aligns with your brand ethos and communicates effectively to your target audience.

Key Points to Consider:

1. **Industry Alignment**: Identify templates tailored to your specific industry for a more relevant and professional appearance.

2. **Design Variety**: Explore the diverse designs within each theme to find a template that stands out and represents your unique style.

3. **Mobile Responsiveness**: Ensure the chosen template is optimized for mobile devices to reach a broader audience.

Selecting a Template Based on Needs

Selecting the right template is a crucial decision that sets the tone for your entire website. This process involves considering your business goals, target audience, and the functionality you require. Each template comes with its own set of features, so it's essential to align these with your objectives.

To add a burst of decisiveness to the selection process, start by defining the primary purpose of your website. Are you selling products, showcasing a portfolio, or providing information? Once you have a clear objective, browse through the templates and focus on those that fulfill your specific requirements.

Key Considerations:

1. **Functionality**: Choose a template that supports the features you need, whether it's e-commerce capabilities, blog integration, or multimedia support.

2. **Scalability**: Consider your future needs. Opt for a template that allows for easy scalability as your business or online presence grows.

3. **User Experience**: Prioritize templates that offer an intuitive user experience, ensuring that visitors can navigate your site effortlessly.

By delving into the intricacies of each template and aligning them with your goals, the process of selecting the perfect WIX template becomes a thoughtful and purpose-driven endeavor.

Customizing Templates

Now that you've chosen the ideal template as your canvas, the next step involves making it uniquely yours through customization. WIX provides a user-friendly interface that empowers users to edit text, images, and overall design elements seamlessly. Let's unravel the art of customizing templates to reflect your brand identity.

Editing Text and Images

Customizing the textual and visual components of your chosen template allows you to tailor the content to your brand voice and aesthetics. WIX's drag-and-drop editor simplifies this process, making it accessible to users with varying levels of technical expertise.

Key Steps:

1. **Textual Edits**: Update the default text with compelling and concise copy that resonates with your audience.

2. **Image Replacement**: Swap placeholder images with high-quality visuals that align with your brand imagery.

3. **Font and Color Adjustments**: Fine-tune the font styles and color schemes to match your brand guidelines.

By infusing your personality into the template through these edits, you transform it from a generic design into a digital representation of your brand story.

Incorporating Personal Branding

To elevate your website further, go beyond the basics of text and image edits. Incorporate personal branding elements to establish a cohesive and memorable online identity.

Key Branding Elements:

1. **Logo Integration**: Place your logo prominently for instant brand recognition.

2. **Color Consistency**: Ensure consistency in color schemes across your website to reinforce brand cohesion.

3. **Unique Features**: Explore WIX's additional features, such as animations or interactive elements, to add a personalized touch.

Remember, customization isn't just about aesthetics; it's about creating an online space that authentically represents your brand values and engages your audience effectively.

BUILDING YOUR WEBSITE

Adding Pages

C reating a website involves more than just design; it requires thoughtful consideration of the pages that make up its structure. The homepage is the virtual storefront, the face of the brand, and crafting it effectively is paramount. Home, the initial point of contact, should be welcoming and reflective of the brand's identity. It must provide a quick overview of the website's purpose and offerings, captivating visitors from the first glance. About Us delves into the brand's story, fostering a connection with the audience. It should communicate the brand's values, mission, and vision, building trust and credibility.

Contact is the bridge between the virtual and real world, allowing users to reach out. The importance of a user-friendly contact page cannot be overstated. Ensure it includes various contact methods, such as email, phone, or a contact form. **Services or Products** pages provide detailed information on what the brand offers. It's an opportunity to showcase the features, benefits, and unique selling points, helping visitors make informed decisions. Lastly, **Blog** or **News** pages keep the content fresh and engage the audience. Regular updates showcase expertise, boost SEO, and keep visitors returning.

Understanding the importance of page structure is pivotal. It determines the user experience and influences search engine rankings. **Navigation menus** should be intuitive, guiding visitors seamlessly through the website. Prioritize a clear hierarchy, ensuring essential pages are easily accessible. Consistent branding elements, such as logos and color schemes, should be maintained across all pages, fostering brand recognition. Proper use of headings and subheadings aids readability, making the content digestible.

In essence, adding pages is not a mere formality but a strategic process that shapes the user's journey and perception of the brand.

Incorporating Media

The visual appeal of a website is often the first thing users notice, making the incorporation of media a critical aspect of web design. **Images** are powerful tools for conveying information and eliciting emotions. High-quality, relevant images can significantly enhance the overall aesthetic and user experience. However, it's crucial to optimize images for web use to prevent slow loading times, a major factor in user satisfaction.

Videos, on the other hand, bring dynamic content that can explain complex concepts or showcase products in action. With the prevalence of high-speed internet, embedding videos has become commonplace. Still, it's essential to strike a balance, as too many videos can overwhelm users.

Best practices for visual content involve maintaining a cohesive visual identity. Consistent image quality, style, and tone contribute to a professional appearance. Consider the relevance of each image or video to the content it accompanies, ensuring a seamless integration that enhances rather than distracts. Alt text for images is not only an accessibility feature but also a valuable SEO tool.

Accessibility is paramount when incorporating media. Provide alternative formats or descriptions for users with disabilities, ensuring an inclusive experience. Responsive design is another key consideration, ensuring that images and videos adapt to different screen sizes for a consistent experience across devices.

In summary, the strategic use of media can elevate a website's appeal and engagement, but careful consideration of quality, relevance, and accessibility is crucial.

Integrating Apps and Plugins

To enhance a website's functionality, integrating third-party apps and plugins is a common practice. However, this process requires thoughtful consideration to avoid potential issues and ensure a seamless user experience.

Enhancing functionality with third-party apps opens up a world of possibilities. From e-commerce tools to social media integrations, apps can add features that cater to specific needs. However, it's essential to prioritize apps that align with the website's goals and user expectations. Unnecessary or conflicting apps can clutter the interface and compromise performance.

When it comes to plugins, selecting and installing them requires a strategic approach. **Tips for selecting plugins** include researching their reputation, user reviews, and compatibility with the website platform. Choose plugins from reputable developers to minimize security risks and ensure ongoing support and updates. Always check for compatibility with the website's theme and other plugins to prevent conflicts.

Installing plugins should be approached with caution. While they can enhance functionality, an excess of plugins can slow down the website and lead to security vulnerabilities. Regularly update plugins to patch security flaws and ensure optimal performance. Additionally, deactivate and delete any unused plugins to declutter the backend and reduce the risk of conflicts.

DESIGN TIPS FOR BEGINNERS

Color and Font Selection

I n the realm of web design, the selection of colors and fonts plays a pivotal role in shaping the overall aesthetics and functionality of a website. The art of combining colors and fonts is not just about personal preference; it involves a deep understanding of the psychological impact each element can have on users. To achieve a visually appealing and effective design, designers need to consider factors such as contrast, harmony, and readability.

1. Contrast in Colors: Choosing colors that provide an adequate level of contrast is essential for readability and accessibility. High contrast between text and background ensures that users can easily distinguish content, enhancing the overall user experience. It's crucial to strike a balance—too much contrast can be overwhelming, while too little can lead to readability issues.

2. Harmonious Color Schemes: Creating a cohesive

color palette involves selecting hues that work well together. Color harmony can be achieved through various methods, such as complementary, analogous, or triadic color schemes. The right combination of colors not only enhances the visual appeal but also conveys the desired emotions and brand identity.

3. Readable Fonts: Font selection is equally important when it comes to user experience. Readability should be a top priority, especially considering the diverse range of devices users might use to access the website. Sans-serif fonts are often recommended for online content due to their clean and legible appearance on screens. It's vital to choose fonts that align with the brand's personality while ensuring they are easy to read in different sizes and formats.

4. Font Size and Line Spacing: Ensuring readability extends beyond selecting the right font; font size and line spacing also play crucial roles. Adequate font size, especially for body text, is essential for comfortable reading. Proper line spacing prevents text from feeling cramped, enhancing the overall readability of the content.

5. Brand Consistency: Consistency is key when it comes to color and font selection. Establishing a brand's visual identity requires maintaining a consistent color palette and font usage across all platforms. This uniformity not only enhances brand recognition but also contributes to a professional and polished appearance.

Creating a Cohesive Design Palette

A cohesive design palette is the foundation of a visually appealing and effective website. It goes beyond choosing colors that look good together; it involves creating a harmonious visual language that aligns with the brand's identity and resonates with the target audience.

1. Brand Identity: The design palette should reflect the essence of the brand. Understanding the brand's values, target audience, and overall personality is crucial in selecting colors that convey the right message. Consistency in color usage across different elements of the website reinforces the brand identity.

2. Limited Color Palette: While it might be tempting to use a wide range of colors, simplicity often reigns supreme in design. Limiting the color palette to a few key hues creates a more cohesive and focused visual experience. A well-chosen limited palette not only looks sophisticated but also makes it easier for users to navigate and understand the content.

3. Color Psychology: Colors evoke emotions and can influence user behavior. It's essential to consider the psychological impact of each color when creating a design palette. Warm colors like red and orange can convey energy and excitement, while cool colors like blue and green can evoke calmness and trust. Understanding color psychology enables designers to make intentional choices that align with the website's goals.

4. Accessibility: A cohesive design palette should also take into account accessibility considerations. Ensuring that color choices meet accessibility standards ensures that the website is inclusive and can be easily navigated by users with visual impairments. Providing sufficient color contrast and using alternative indicators for information conveyance are crucial aspects of creating an accessible design palette.

5. Visual Hierarchy: The design palette should contribute to establishing a clear visual hierarchy on the website. Using contrasting colors for important elements, such as call-to-action buttons or headings, helps guide users through the content. A well-defined visual hierarchy enhances user engagement and ensures that key messages are communicated effectively.

Choosing Readable Fonts

The selection of readable fonts is a fundamental aspect of web design that directly impacts user engagement and satisfaction. Users should be able to consume content effortlessly, and the right font choices contribute significantly to achieving this goal.

1. Font Legibility: Legibility is the foremost consideration when choosing fonts for a website. While artistic and decorative fonts may have their place, they are often unsuitable for body text. Sans-serif fonts are generally preferred for online content due to their clean lines and simplicity, which enhances readability on screens.

2. Responsive Font Design: Given the variety of devices used to access websites, fonts must be responsive. Responsive font design ensures that text remains readable across different screen sizes and resolutions. This involves selecting fonts that scale well and adjusting font sizes to maintain optimal readability on various devices.

3. Font Pairing: Combining fonts effectively can contribute to a visually interesting and dynamic design. However, it's crucial to strike a balance between contrast and harmony. Bold and decorative fonts can be paired with more neutral and readable fonts to create a hierarchy and emphasize key elements without sacrificing readability.

4. Variable Fonts: The use of variable fonts is a modern approach to responsive design. Variable fonts allow for dynamic adjustments in weight, width, and other attributes, providing flexibility in adapting to different devices and screen sizes. Incorporating variable fonts can enhance the overall user experience by ensuring consistent readability.

5. Testing Across Devices: Even after careful font selection, it's essential to test the chosen fonts across various devices and browsers. Differences in rendering can affect the overall appearance and readability. Regular testing ensures that the selected fonts perform well and maintain optimal readability across the diverse landscape of web users.

Layout and Organization

The layout and organization of a website are critical factors that contribute to user satisfaction and engagement. A well-organized and user-friendly layout enhances the overall user experience, making it easy for visitors to navigate, find information, and interact with the content.

1. Intuitive Navigation: The navigation structure should be intuitive and user-friendly. Users should be able to easily locate essential information without feeling overwhelmed. Clear menus, logical categorization, and a straightforward navigation flow contribute to a positive user experience.

2. Consistent Design Elements: Consistency in design elements, such as headers, footers, and navigation bars, helps users orient themselves within the website. Uniformity in layout across different pages creates a sense of coherence and makes it easier for users to understand and predict where to find specific information.

3. Mobile Responsiveness: With an increasing number of users accessing websites on mobile devices, ensuring mobile responsiveness is paramount. A responsive layout adapts seamlessly to different screen sizes, providing an optimal viewing experience across desktops, tablets, and smartphones.

4. Focused Content Blocks: Breaking down content into focused and visually distinct blocks improves readability and engagement. Each content block should have a clear purpose, and the overall layout should guide users through a logical sequence of information. Visual cues, such as headings and imagery, help users navigate through the content effortlessly.

5. User Testing: User testing is a crucial step in evaluating the effectiveness of a website's layout and organization. Gathering feedback from real users helps identify pain points, areas of confusion, and opportunities for improvement.

OPTIMIZING FOR SEARCH ENGINES

Introduction to SEO

S earch Engine Optimization, commonly known as SEO, is a multifaceted and dynamic field that plays a crucial role in enhancing the online presence of websites. In a world where digital visibility is paramount, understanding the fundamentals of SEO is essential for individuals and businesses alike. At its core, SEO involves optimizing a website's content, structure, and overall online footprint to ensure it ranks higher in search engine results. This introductory guide aims to unravel the intricacies of SEO, providing a foundation for those looking to delve into the world of digital marketing.

SEO encompasses various strategies and techniques geared towards making a website more accessible to search engines like Google, Bing, and Yahoo. The primary goal is to increase the likelihood of the website appearing on the first page of search results, thereby driving organic traffic. Understanding how search engines operate is fundamental to SEO. They employ complex algorithms that analyze numerous factors to determine the relevance and quality of a website's content. Keywords, backlinks, and user experience are among the many elements that influence search engine rankings.

Importance of SEO for Websites

The significance of SEO for websites cannot be overstated. In a digital landscape saturated with information, a well-optimized website stands a better chance of reaching its target audience. Here are several key reasons why SEO is crucial for the success of any online platform:

1. Enhanced Visibility:

- SEO significantly improves a website's visibility on search engines.
- Higher visibility translates to increased chances of attracting organic traffic.

2. Credibility and Trust:

- Websites that appear on the first page of search results are often perceived as more trustworthy and credible by users.
- Establishing trust is vital for converting visitors into customers or followers.

3. Targeted Traffic:

- SEO allows businesses to target specific keywords relevant to their industry.
- This targeted approach ensures that the traffic generated is more likely to convert.

4. Improved User Experience:

- SEO involves optimizing the website's structure and content, leading to a better user experience.
- A positive user experience contributes to lower bounce rates and increased engagement.

Basic SEO Practices for WIX

WIX, a popular website builder, empowers users to create stunning websites with ease. However, to ensure these websites perform well in search engine rankings, implementing basic SEO practices is essential. Here's a breakdown of fundamental SEO practices tailored for WIX users:

1. Keyword Research:

- Identify relevant keywords related to your website's content and target audience.
- Utilize tools like Google Keyword Planner to discover high-impact keywords.

2. On-Page Optimization:

- Optimize page titles, meta descriptions, and headers with chosen keywords.
- Ensure that your content is well-structured, including the use of headings and subheadings.

3. Quality Content Creation:

- Regularly update your website with high-quality, relevant content.
- Engaging content not only attracts visitors but also encourages them to spend more time on your site.

4. Mobile-Friendly Design:

- WIX offers mobile-responsive templates, but it's crucial to ensure your website looks great and functions well on various devices.
- Google prioritizes mobile-friendly websites in its rankings.

5. Image Optimization:

- Compress images to improve website loading speed.
- Use descriptive file names and alt tags to optimize images for search engines.

Utilizing WIX SEO Tools

WIX provides users with a range of built-in SEO tools to streamline the optimization process. Leveraging these tools can significantly boost your website's visibility. Here's an exploration of key WIX SEO features:

1. WIX SEO Wiz:

- The WIX SEO Wiz is a step-by-step guide that assists users in optimizing their websites.
- It provides personalized SEO plans based on the user's goals and industry.

2. Page SEO Settings:

- WIX allows users to customize SEO settings for individual pages.
- This includes meta tags, URL structures, and social media sharing information.

3. Site Analytics:

- WIX offers an integrated analytics tool to monitor website performance.
- Track key metrics like traffic, visitor demographics, and popular content.

4. XML Sitemap:

- WIX automatically generates XML sitemaps for websites, making it easier for search engines to crawl and index content.
- Ensure your sitemap is up-to-date and submitted

to search engine consoles.

Step-by-Step Guide to WIX SEO Features

Now, let's delve into a step-by-step guide on how to effectively use WIX SEO features to optimize your website:

1. Access WIX SEO Wiz:

- Log in to your WIX account and find the SEO Wiz in the dashboard.
- Follow the prompts to input information about your website, business, and goals.

2. Customize Page SEO Settings:

- For each page, access the SEO settings.
- Input unique meta titles, descriptions, and URLs for optimal search engine visibility.

3. Connect to Google Analytics:

- Integrate your WIX website with Google Analytics for in-depth performance tracking.
- This connection provides valuable insights into user behavior and site traffic.

4. Regularly Update Content:

- Keep your website content fresh and relevant.
- Utilize the WIX Blog app to publish regular posts that align with your target keywords.

5. Utilize WIX SEO Apps:

- Explore WIX App Market for additional SEO tools and apps.
- These apps can enhance your website's functionality and SEO performance.

Improving Website Visibility

Improving website visibility is an ongoing process that

requires consistent effort and optimization. Here are actionable tips to enhance the visibility of your website:

1. Monitor Analytics:

- Regularly review website analytics to identify areas for improvement.
- Adjust your SEO strategy based on the performance data.

2. Build Quality Backlinks:

- Earn backlinks from reputable websites in your industry.
- High-quality backlinks contribute to your website's authority and search engine rankings.

3. Social Media Integration:

- Leverage social media platforms to promote your content.
- Social signals positively impact search engine rankings.

4. User Engagement:

- Encourage user engagement through comments, shares, and social media interactions.
- Engaged users are more likely to become loyal visitors.

PREVIEWING AND PUBLISHING YOUR WEBSITE

Reviewing the Website

When it comes to creating a website, the initial excitement of design and content creation can sometimes overshadow the critical step of reviewing the website before it goes live. A comprehensive review ensures that your website is not only visually appealing but also functional and error-free. Start by checking for typographical errors and grammatical mistakes. These seemingly minor issues can significantly impact the professionalism of your website. Next, pay attention to the overall consistency in design. Fonts, colors, and images should harmonize to create a cohesive look and feel.

As you review, scrutinize the navigation elements. Ensure that all **links are working correctly**, leading visitors to the intended pages. Broken links can frustrate users and negatively impact your website's SEO. Consider the **user experience** by navigating through your site as if you were a visitor. Are there any confusing or convoluted paths? Make sure the journey through your website is intuitive and straightforward.

Additionally, pay special attention to how your website appears on different browsers. **Cross-browser compatibility** is crucial to reach a broader audience. What looks fantastic on one browser might appear distorted on another. Testing on multiple browsers can help you identify and address any discrepancies.

Lastly, check the loading speed of your pages. A slow website can lead to a high bounce rate as users may not have the patience to wait for content to load. Tools like Google PageSpeed Insights can provide insights into areas for improvement.

Checking for errors and consistency

Digging deeper into the review process involves a meticulous check for errors and consistency. Beyond the surface-level typos, consider the **consistency of tone and messaging** across all pages. Inconsistencies can confuse visitors and dilute your brand identity. Create a checklist of key messages and ensure they are consistently communicated throughout your website.

Focus on the **functionality of interactive elements** such as forms, buttons, and menus. Check that forms are submitting data correctly, buttons are responsive, and menus are functioning as expected. These elements are crucial for user engagement and should be thoroughly tested to avoid any potential issues.

For a comprehensive review, it's essential to examine your

website's **compatibility with different devices**. Test your site on various devices, including smartphones and tablets, to ensure a seamless experience for users regardless of the device they use. Mobile responsiveness is no longer an option—it's a necessity for reaching today's diverse online audience.

Ensuring mobile responsiveness

In an era where mobile devices dominate internet usage, ensuring your website is mobile-responsive is paramount. Google prioritizes mobile-friendly websites in its search rankings, making it crucial for SEO. To achieve this, employ a **responsive design approach**. This means your website adapts seamlessly to different screen sizes, providing an optimal user experience on both desktop and mobile devices.

Start by checking the layout of your website on a mobile screen. Ensure that all elements, including images, text, and buttons, are displayed correctly and are easily clickable. **Optimize images for mobile devices** to improve loading times without compromising quality. Large images can slow down the loading speed, adversely affecting user experience.

Test navigation on mobile devices. The menu should be accessible and easy to use, and links should lead to the correct pages. Consider implementing touch-friendly features, such as larger buttons, to accommodate mobile users. Mobile responsiveness is not just about fitting content onto a smaller screen; it's about providing a seamless and enjoyable experience for users on the go.

In summary, reviewing your website is a crucial step in ensuring a successful online presence. Pay attention to details, be consistent, and prioritize mobile responsiveness to cater to the diverse ways users access the internet.

Publishing Your WIX Website

After the meticulous process of designing and reviewing your website, the next step is to publish it for the world to see. WIX, a popular website builder, makes this process relatively straightforward. Here's a step-by-step guide to taking your WIX website live.

1. **Final Checks**: Before publishing, conduct a final review of your website. Ensure all elements are in place, and there are no last-minute changes needed. Verify that your contact forms and interactive elements function correctly.

2. **Custom Domain**: If you haven't already, consider purchasing a custom domain for your website. This not only adds a professional touch but also makes it easier for visitors to remember your web address.

3. **Publish Button**: In your WIX dashboard, locate the "Publish" button. Clicking on this button will make your website accessible to the public. WIX offers a free subdomain, but if you have a custom domain, your website will be published under that.

4. **SEO Settings**: Optimize your website for search engines by adjusting the SEO settings. Add relevant meta tags, descriptions, and keywords to improve your site's visibility on search engine results pages.

5. **Social Media Integration**: Connect your social media accounts to your WIX website. This allows

visitors to easily share your content on various platforms, expanding your online reach.

6. **SSL Certificate**: Enable the SSL certificate for your website to ensure a secure connection. This is crucial for building trust with your audience, especially if your website involves transactions or the collection of sensitive information.

7. **Mobile Preview**: Before finalizing the publishing process, use WIX's mobile preview feature to ensure your website looks and functions well on different devices.

Step-by-step guide to going live

Now that your website is live, there are additional steps to enhance its performance and reach. Consider the following guide to further optimize your online presence.

1. **Monitor Analytics**: Use tools like Google Analytics to track the performance of your website. Analyze user behavior, traffic sources, and popular content. This data can guide future improvements and content strategies.

2. **Regular Updates**: Keep your website content fresh by regularly updating information, blog posts, or product listings. This not only provides value to visitors but also improves your search engine rankings.

3. **Engage with Visitors**: Encourage user interaction through comments, forums, or social media integration. Engaging with your audience builds a sense of community and loyalty.

4. **Optimize for Speed**: Continuously monitor and

optimize your website's loading speed. This is crucial for retaining visitors and improving your search engine rankings.

5. **Back-Up Your Website**: Regularly back up your website to prevent data loss in case of unexpected issues. Many website builders, including WIX, offer automatic backup solutions.

Tips for promoting your website

Once your website is live and optimized, the next challenge is to promote it effectively. Here are some tips to boost the visibility and reach of your WIX website.

1. **Social Media Marketing**: Leverage social media platforms to promote your website. Create engaging posts, share relevant content, and interact with your audience. Social media is a powerful tool for driving traffic and building a community around your brand.

2. **Email Marketing**: Build an email list and use newsletters to keep your audience informed about updates, promotions, or new content on your website. Email marketing remains a reliable method for nurturing customer relationships.

3. **Collaborate with Influencers**: Identify influencers or bloggers in your niche and explore collaboration opportunities. Influencer marketing can introduce your website to a wider audience and build credibility.

4. **Paid Advertising**: Consider using paid advertising, such as Google Ads or social media ads, to target specific demographics and increase visibility. Allocate a budget for advertising based

on your business goals.

5. **Optimize for SEO**: Continuously optimize your website for search engines. Research and use relevant keywords, create high-quality content, and build backlinks to improve your website's ranking on search engine results pages.

CONCLUSION

Recap of Key Takeaways

U nderstanding and summarizing key takeaways from any experience or learning is crucial for solidifying knowledge and implementing insights effectively. It allows individuals to distill complex information into manageable points for better retention and application. In this section, we will delve into the significance of recapping key takeaways and explore strategies to enhance this process.

Recapping involves revisiting the core concepts, main ideas, and pivotal learnings from a particular experience or study. This practice is essential in various fields, including education, business, and personal development. **Key takeaways serve as the foundation for informed decision-making, problem-solving, and continuous improvement.**

Importance of Recap

1. **Consolidation of Information:** Recapitulating key takeaways aids in consolidating information.

It enables individuals to connect dots, identify patterns, and develop a comprehensive understanding of the subject matter.

2. **Enhanced Retention:** Repetition is a powerful tool for memory enhancement. By revisiting key takeaways, individuals reinforce their memory, making it easier to recall information when needed.

3. **Application in Decision-Making:** Recapitulating key points equips individuals with the necessary insights to make informed decisions. It ensures that lessons learned are applied in practical scenarios.

4. **Facilitation of Communication:** Communicating ideas effectively requires a clear understanding of key concepts. Recapitulation enables individuals to articulate their thoughts coherently, fostering better communication.

Strategies for Effective Recap

1. **Organized Note-Taking:** Taking organized and structured notes during the learning process enhances the recapitulation process. Categorizing information and using visual aids can make the recap more efficient.

2. **Active Reflection:** Engaging in active reflection is crucial for effective recap. This involves thinking critically about the material, asking questions, and connecting new information to existing knowledge.

3. **Periodic Reviews:** Instead of cramming information, periodic reviews spread over

time enhance long-term retention. Set specific intervals to revisit key takeaways to reinforce learning.

4. **Interactive Discussions:** Engaging in discussions with peers or mentors provides a platform to share and gain insights. Explaining key takeaways to others reinforces understanding and may offer different perspectives.

Encouragement for Beginners

Embarking on a new journey, whether it be learning a new skill, pursuing a passion, or entering a new industry, can be both exciting and daunting, especially for beginners. This section aims to provide encouragement for those starting their ventures, emphasizing the importance of perseverance, resilience, and continuous learning.

Challenges Faced by Beginners

1. **Overcoming the Learning Curve:** Every new endeavor comes with a learning curve. Beginners may feel overwhelmed by the sheer volume of information and skills they need to acquire.

2. **Dealing with Imposter Syndrome:** Imposter syndrome is common among beginners. It involves doubting one's abilities and feeling like a fraud. Recognizing and overcoming this mindset is crucial for growth.

3. **Managing Frustration:** Setbacks and challenges are inevitable. Beginners need to learn how to manage frustration and view obstacles as opportunities for learning and improvement.

4. **Balancing Enthusiasm and Realism:** While enthusiasm is essential, beginners should also maintain a realistic outlook. Setting achievable goals and celebrating small victories can contribute to long-term success.

Words of Encouragement

1. **Embrace the Learning Process:** Learning is a continuous journey. Embrace the process, acknowledging that improvement takes time. Celebrate small victories along the way.

2. **Seek Guidance and Mentorship:** Don't hesitate to seek guidance from experienced individuals in the field. Mentorship can provide valuable insights, guidance, and motivation.

3. **Build a Supportive Community:** Surround yourself with a supportive community of like-minded individuals. Sharing experiences and challenges with others can create a sense of camaraderie and motivation.

4. **Embrace Failure as a Stepping Stone:** Failure is not the end but a stepping stone to success. Learn from mistakes, adapt, and use setbacks as opportunities for growth.

www.ingramcontent.com/pod-product-compliance
Lightning Source LLC
LaVergne TN
LVHW051751050326
832903LV00029B/2854